Why Is This Festival Special?

Id-ul-Fitr

Jillian Powell

A⁺
DISCARD
Smart Apple Media

First published in 2005 by Franklin Watts
96 Leonard Street, London EC2A 4XD

Franklin Watts Australia
Level 17/207 Kent Street, Sydney NSW 2000

Note: When Muslims say the name of one of the prophets, they always say afterward "Peace Be Upon Him," which is shown in this book as "pbuh."

Series editor: Sarah Peutrill, Art director: Jonathan Hair, Designer: Ian Thompson, Picture researcher: Diana Morris, Consultant: Ghulam Sarwar, Director of the Muslim Education Trust, London

Picture credits: Muhammed Bazuki/Reuters/Corbis: 7, 10b. Marco Brivio/Alamy: 17t. Juliet Highet/Ark Religion: 24. Image Works/Topfoto: 21t. Ali Jarekji/Reuters/Corbis: 8. C. Rennie/Ark Religion: 16. Helene Rogers/Ark Religion: 9, 19b, 20b, 25t. Roshan Sharma/Photographers Direct: front cover t, 10c. World Religions Picture Library: 3, 6, 12, 13b, 15t, 15b, 18b, 22, 23t, 23b, 25b, 26, 27t, 27b. A. Zerbaigan/Topfoto: 11.

Published in the United States by Smart Apple Media
2140 Howard Drive West, North Mankato, Minnesota 56003

U.S. publication copyright © 2007 Smart Apple Media

Library of Congress Cataloging-in-Publication Data

Powell, Jillian.
Id-ul-fitr / by Jillian Powell.
p. cm. — (Why is this festival special?)
Includes index.
ISBN-13 : 978-1-58340-943-5
1. Id-ul-Fitr—Juvenile literature. 2. Islam—Customs and practices—Juvenile literature. I. Title.

BP186.45.P68 2006
297.3'6—dc22   2005052551

9 8 7 6 5 4 3 2 1

Contents

A happy festival

Id-ul-Fitr is a Muslim festival. Muslims are people who follow a religion called Islam. They believe in one God, called Allah.

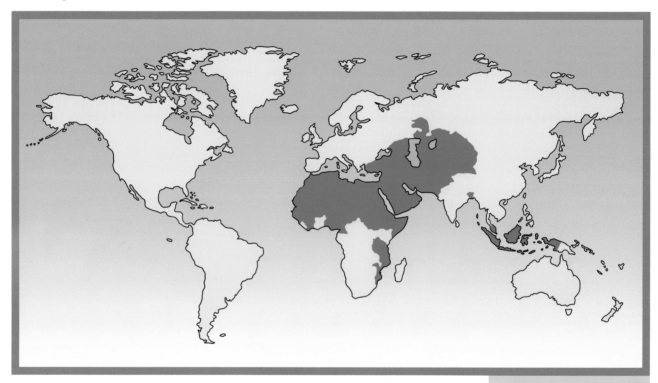

Muslims study their holy book, the Koran, and try to live their lives doing what Allah wants them to do.

Islam is the main religion of more than 60 countries. The countries where more than half of the people are Muslim are shown in green.

In Muslim countries, Muslim children read the Koran in school as well as at home.

Id-ul-Fitr (often called just Id) celebrates the end of Ramadan, a holy month when most Muslims fast. Fasting means they do not eat, drink, or smoke in the daytime.

Id is a time for giving thanks to Allah, celebrating with family and friends, and making other people happy.

Id-ul-Fitr is celebrated for one day.

"At the start of Id, we all wish each other 'Id Mubarak,' which means Happy Festival."
Shaheen, age 10

A young Malaysian girl plays with a sparkler on the eve of the Id celebrations.

Ramadan

Ramadan is a time for fasting.

Ramadan is the ninth month in the Islamic calendar (see page 29). It is a very holy month. It begins when the new moon is seen.

During Ramadan, Muslims go without food and water all day. They eat only before dawn and after sunset.

The new moon is when the moon first appears as a crescent in the sky.

A Muslim family prays before sharing a meal together before dawn.

Fasting is important to Muslims. It helps them to show that they are thinking about Allah and that they can be strong and go without food.

Most Muslims fast except for the old or sick, young children, and women who are having babies.

When the next new moon is seen, Ramadan ends, and Id begins.

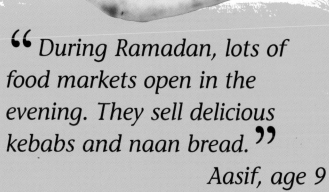

" During Ramadan, lots of food markets open in the evening. They sell delicious kebabs and naan bread. "

Aasif, age 9

Getting ready

Families enjoy getting ready for the Id celebrations.

Everyone is busy as the festival of Id gets nearer. Many people like to clean and paint their homes. They hang up decorations such as flowers, balloons, and streamers, as well as banners that say "Id Mubarak."

A Muslim woman buying artificial flowers to decorate her home before Id.

In Muslim countries, markets and shops stay open late during the last weeks of Ramadan.

Muslims buy cards and presents, and food for the family feast that takes place when the fast ends.

Malaysians buy food for the Id feast at a busy market.

Families get excited as they wait to see the new moon so they can start celebrating. Many Muslims call their mosque to find out if the new moon has been seen in the evening sky.

" *Dad calls the mosque to find out when Id has started. We are allowed to stay up late for the start of Id.* "

Sameera, age 10

Mosques are places where Muslims meet to study and to pray to Allah.

Prayers

Id is a time for prayer and thanksgiving. On the morning of Id, everyone gets up early to go to the mosque for prayers.

Before going into the mosque, people must wash.

Then they go into the prayer hall. The men and boys gather in one area, and the women and girls in another.

Mosques are always full, and many people pray outside in the courtyard as well. In hot countries, Id prayers may be held in a park or field.

Muslim men wash in a special area before entering the mosque.

The imam leads special prayers at Id. Muslims use prayer mats and pray facing toward Mecca. This is the city in Saudi Arabia where Muhammad (pbuh), Islam's last and most important prophet, was born.

"When we are praying, I stay next to Dad so I can copy what he does."

Husain, age 9

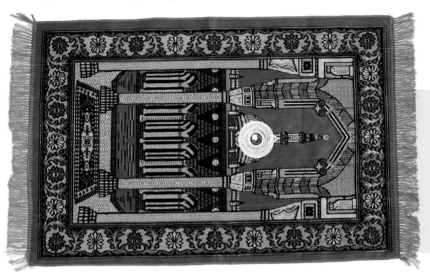

This is a prayer mat that a Muslim might use when traveling. It has a compass, which makes it easy to tell which way faces toward Mecca.

Everyone says "Thank you" to Allah and asks Him to help them follow a good Muslim life. Then the imam gives a sermon.

Muslims listen to a sermon for Id in their mosque.

After prayers, everyone goes outside to start celebrating with family and friends.

The Koran

The Koran is an important part of Ramadan.

The Koran is the holy book of Islam. It tells Muslims how Allah wants them to live their lives and sets out the rules of Islam. During Ramadan and Id, Muslims try to spend lots of time reading the Koran.

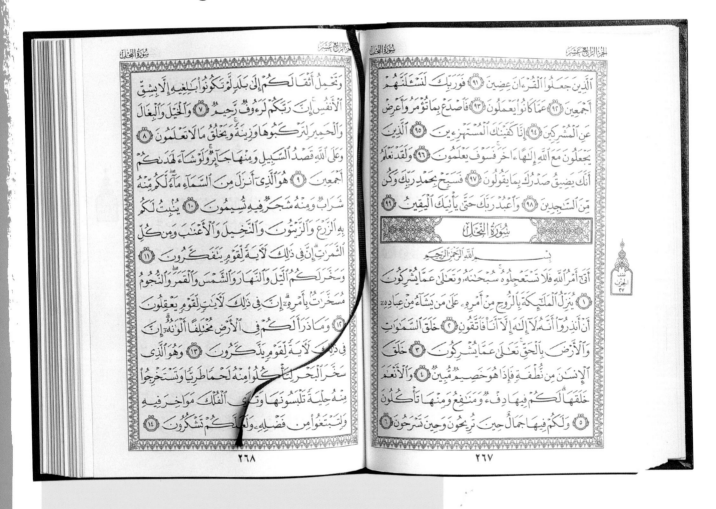

The Koran is written in Arabic. Some people read the Koran in their own language, but they try to learn to read it in Arabic, too.

These Muslim children are answering their teacher's questions on the Koran.

> " We have special classes after school to learn the Koran. We had to learn the Arabic alphabet first. "
>
> Imran, age 9

In some countries, such as Malaysia and countries in East Africa, there are competitions at Id in which people stand up and recite parts of the Koran that they have learned by heart.

Muslim children learn to read and remember words from the Koran.

Sharing and forgiveness

Id is a time for thinking of others.

Muslims believe that Id is a time to be kind to others and to forgive people who have done something to upset you.

They also believe that Id is a time for sharing and giving. They collect money to give to charity so that everyone can enjoy the Id celebrations. This is called Zakat-ul-Fitr.

▶ This mosque has a Zakat box, in which Muslims can put money to help the poor.

Muslims try to give the amount of money that would buy a meal for each person in their family.

People give the money before prayers on the morning of Id. Often the money is collected at a mosque, so it can be shared right away and used to buy meals for the poor at Id.

A Muslim father teaches his son to give Zakat.

" My brothers and I all save our allowance money for Zakat at Id. We put it into a big box at the mosque. "
Mohammed, age 9

Children save their allowance money so they can give, too.

Children can use a money box to save for Zakat.

Clothes for Id

On Id morning, families get up early, and everyone takes a bath or shower.

Muslims must wash before going to prayer. Many women and men put on a special perfume for Id.

> Perfume is often given as a gift at Id. The Prophet Muhammad (pbuh) liked perfume and encouraged its use.

It is important for Muslims to look their best for the festival. People like to dress up in their best clothes. Some buy new clothes for the celebrations. Men and boys often dress in white, which is the color of purity.

Muslim women and children dressed for Id.

18

Many women and girls paint their hands with henna, in pretty patterns called mehndi. This is traditional for special occasions and festivals. Sometimes they buy new jewelry to wear at Id, too.

" My aunt buys henna to do mehndi at Id. She draws patterns for my sisters and me. "
Fatimah, age 10

This Muslim woman is having her hands painted for Id at a market.

Cards and gifts

Muslims give cards and gifts to celebrate Id.

These Id cards show pictures of mosques.

In the days before Id, people buy greeting cards wishing "Id Mubarak" to send to their family and friends.

Children often make their own cards for Id at school.

Children may decorate their Id cards with pretty patterns and sometimes words from the Koran.

Many Muslims visit their relatives at Id, after they leave the mosque. Family is important to most Muslims, and relatives like to gather to celebrate Id as a group.

Families unwrap their presents together. Children may receive gifts of new clothes, toys, or candy. They are often given money at Id, too.

Grandparents like to give their grandchildren presents at Id.

" My grandparents give us little bags of candy at Id. We buy them things for the home like special decorations. "

Shakil, age 9

Food and family meals

Food is an important part of Id.

On the morning of Id, it is traditional to end the fast of Ramadan with fresh dates and a sweet drink.

Later, families enjoy a big midday dinner. This is the first meal they have eaten in the daytime for a month.

Muslim women in Oman cook a big meal for Id.

22

Sweet foods, such as stuffed dates or figs, are popular at Id, as are spicy puddings made with rice or pasta and sweet milk.

Dishes for Id include sweet milk pudding and dried fruits.

66 *Mom bakes lots of delicious sweets for Id. I like helping her in the kitchen.* 99
Fatimah, age 10

After the meal, everyone hugs each other three times as a sign of brotherhood and sisterhood and closeness to each other.

Two sisters hug each other after their family meal at Id.

23

Fun and fairs

Id is celebrated with fairs and street parades.

After the midday dinner, many people like to go out and have fun. In some Muslim countries, there are street parades in which people wear colorful robes and turbans.

These Nigerians are celebrating Id with singing and drumming.

Many cities and towns hold markets and fairs for the festival. There are stalls that sell food, candy, jewelry, gifts, and sometimes fun fair rides for children.

> 66 *Id is exciting because we get to open our presents, then in the afternoon we all go out to the fair.* 99
>
> *Shaheen, age 10*

Some Muslim families enjoy a trip to the fair at Id.

There may be actors putting on plays or shows, people playing music, and groups of acrobats to watch.

A folk artist performing at an Id concert in Pakistan.

Many people also like to hold their own party at Id and invite all of their family and friends.

Sports and games

In Muslim countries, such as Saudi Arabia and Algeria, Id-ul-Fitr is a national holiday. Lots of sports events and races are held.

Horse racing is popular in North Africa and the Middle East.

66 We don't have to go to school at Id. Everyone looks forward to the holiday. 99

Abdullah, age 9

Horse racing is an exciting sport to watch at Id.

There are also camel races in Morocco and Saudi Arabia. Many people travel a long way to bring their camels to race.

Camel racing during Id celebrations.

Polo is a ball sport played by teams of riders.

In Pakistan and other countries, polo is a popular sport to watch at Id. Sometimes tribes or people from different villages compete against each other. They ride horses and sometimes camels.

Glossary

Arabic the language spoken by people living in Arabia and other countries around the world. It is the language of the Koran.

charity giving money to help people in need.

imam a person who leads prayers in a mosque and helps Muslims understand the Koran. It means "leader."

Islam the religion of Muslims, from Allah.

Islamic calendar a calendar that follows the cycle of the moon (unlike a solar calendar, which follows the cycle of the sun).

Koran the Muslim holy book.

Mecca the city in Saudi Arabia in which the Prophet Muhammad (pbuh) was born.

mosque a place where Muslims go to pray.

Muhammad (pbuh) the final prophet sent by Allah to teach people how to live a good life and worship Him. He lived from A.D. 571 to 632.

polo a ball sport played by people on horses.

prayer words said when a person asks for Allah's blessings.

prophet someone chosen by Allah to teach people their religion.

Ramadan the ninth month of the Islamic calendar and the month of fasting.

sermon (khutbah) a talk given by the imam before Friday prayer and after Id prayer.

Zakat-ul-Fitr money given to those in need at Id-ul-Fitr.

Islam

Muslims follow a religion called Islam. There are nearly 1.3 billion Muslims in the world. The Islamic faith began with the first prophet of Allah, Adam—believed to be the first man on Earth. It was completed with the teachings of the Prophet Muhammad (pbuh), the final messenger of Allah.

Beliefs
Muslims believe in one God, called Allah. They learn about His will through their holy book, the Koran. This contains messages that were given to the Prophet Muhammad (pbuh).

Five Pillars
Muslims try to follow the Five Pillars of Islam:
1) to state, knowingly and willingly, their belief in one God, called Allah, and affirm the messengership of the Prophet Muhammad (pbuh) (this is called shahadah)
2) to pray five times a day
3) to give 1/40th of their savings to the poor
4) to fast for 29 or 30 days during Ramadan
5) to travel, at least once, to Mecca, the city in Saudi Arabia in which the Prophet Muhammad (pbuh) was born.

Calendar
Muslims follow the Islamic lunar calendar, which is a calendar based on the cycle of the moon.

There are six important festivals in the Muslim year. Two were introduced by the Prophet Muhammad (pbuh), and four celebrate events in his life. Id means "happiness" in the Arabic language, and Id-ul-Fitr is one of the happiest festivals in the Muslim year.

Index